# ECO ACTION

It's Time to Take Eco Action!

# CLEANING UP TRANSPORTATION

## ROBYN HARDYMAN

CHERITON
CHILDREN'S BOOKS

Published in 2023 by **Cheriton Children's Books**
PO Box 7258, Bridgnorth, Shropshire, WV16 9ET, UK

© 2023 Cheriton Children's Books

First Edition

Author: Robyn Hardyman
Designer: Paul Myerscough
Editor: Jane Brooke
Proofreader: Wendy Scavuzzo
Consultant: David Hawksett, BSc

Picture credits: Cover: Top: Shutterstock/NadyGinzburg; Center: Shutterstock/
Viktoriia Hnatiuk; Bottom: Shutterstock/Maradon 333. Inside: p1: Shutterstock/
Viktoriia Hnatiuk; pp4-5: Shutterstock/Viktoriia Hnatiuk; p6: Shutterstock/Ako
Photography; p7: Shutterstock/Harvepino; p8: Shutterstock/5m3photos; p9:
Shutterstock/Wangkun Jia; p10: Shutterstock/Hywit Dimyadi; p11: Shutterstock/
Cholpan; p13: Shutterstock/Irin-k; p14: Shutterstock/LanaElcova; p15:
Shutterstock/Imagenet; p16: Shutterstock/View Apart; p17: Shutterstock/Kleber
Cordeiro; p18: Shutterstock/Dmitry Chulov; p19: Shutterstock/Sleeping cat; p20:
Shutterstock/Rblfmr; p21: Shutterstock/Casimiro PT; p23: Shutterstock/Gorynvd;
p24: Shutterstock/Motive56; p25: Shutterstock/Vaalaa; p26: Shutterstock/
Steve Mann; p27: Shutterstock/Aappp; p28: Shutterstock/Scharfsinn; p29:
Shutterstock/Surasak Photo; p30: Shutterstock/Frederic Legrand - COMEO; p31:
Shutterstock/Lev Radin; p32: Shutterstock/Rawpixel.com; p34: Shutterstock/
Martinez Studio; p35: Shutterstock/Ethan Daniels; p36: Shutterstock/Ohrim;
p37: Shutterstock/Mrs ya; p38: Oceanbird; p39: Oceanbird; p41: Shutterstock/
Ernie Hounshell; p42: Shutterstock/Allard One; p43: Shutterstock/Audio und
werbung; p44: Shutterstock/Monkey Business Images; p45: Shutterstock/
gonzagon; Throughout: Shutterstock/Voy Ager.

All rights reserved. No part of this book may be reproduced in any form without
permission from the publisher, except by a reviewer.

Printed in China

Please visit our website,
www.cheritonchildrensbooks.com
to see more of our high-quality books.

# CONTENTS

# WHY WE NEED TO TAKE ECO ACTION

We all need to get around. We travel to school, to work, to visit each other, and on vacation. Everything we find in stores and in our homes has been transported, too, usually several times. All the materials that things are made from are transported to factories. Then, the finished goods are transported to their destinations. The world is an incredibly busy place. People and goods are on the move all the time, by road, rail, sea, and air. We expect to be able to buy goods from just about anywhere in the world, at any time. But all that transportation is creating problems for our planet. It simply cannot cope with the damage that our modern way of life is causing.

We all need to consider what effects the transportation we use is having on the **environment**.

## Polluting the Planet

Today, we are damaging our world. We are **polluting** Earth's land, air, and water. Our transportation methods depend too much on **fossil fuels**. We use too much oil to create **gasoline** and **diesel** for our vehicles. Burning gasoline and diesel in our engines creates gases that are harmful to our planet. We pump them out into its **atmosphere**, where they trap heat and cause changes to our **climate**. These climate changes harm the natural world, and they threaten us, too.

## Too Busy

Our dependence on transportation is also harming the environment because of overcrowding. Anyone who has ever tried to drive through a city at peak times knows that. In the United States alone, there are about 290 million cars. The number of miles traveled by vehicles keeps increasing, too, even though one-third of all trips are just 2 miles (3.2 km) or less! That is not **sustainable**. Our roads and cities cannot cope with the volume of traffic, and our planet cannot cope with the **pollution**, either.

## Harmful to Health

Worldwide, air pollution is harming the health of people on the ground, too. That is especially the case in towns and cities, and beside busy highways. Breathing in polluted air can damage almost every part of the body. Scientists say it causes more than 10 million early deaths each year.

It's Time to Take Eco Action!

So, what can we do to stop the damage that transportation is causing? We can take action—eco action! Eco action is activity that helps protect the planet. In this book, you'll discover what actions people are taking to tackle the harmful impact of our transportation networks. You'll also discover what actions you can take to combat these harmful activities. And you'll learn how you can build a green career that will help protect Earth for future generations. Are you ready to take eco action? Then read on!

# CHAPTER 1

# POLLUTING THE LAND

We cannot avoid transportation in the modern world. People love their cars. They love the freedom that having a car gives them. Many people also need a car to get to work or school. Transportation is also necessary to deliver goods to our factories and stores. But the planet is paying a high price for all the transportation on our roads. In the United States, transportation creates about one-third of all the **greenhouse gases** produced. We all need to make changes.

## Pumping Out Pollution

Earth's atmosphere has become polluted with harmful substances. They can harm humans, animals, and plants. So how do cars and trucks cause the pollution? We burn fossil fuels such as oil and gasoline to create the energy that powers engines. However, when we burn those fuels they give off harmful gases, including carbon dioxide ($CO_2$). Those gases are then pumped from our car and truck exhausts into the air.

## Bigger and Bigger

Bigger cars are generally more polluting than smaller cars. Our cars have been getting bigger in recent decades. Sport utility vehicles (SUVs) are popular but, of all cars, they are the worst polluters. They create more harmful **emissions** than smaller cars.

We do not need big cars for most journeys. We need to stop making and buying big, heavy-polluter cars.

## Gas Guzzlers

Large cars such as SUVs burn more fuel than smaller cars. They therefore travel fewer miles on a single gallon of fuel. Many SUVs can travel only around 20 miles (32.2 km) on 1 gallon (3.8 l) of gasoline. Smaller cars can travel more than 55 miles (88.5 km) on 1 gallon. Burning less fuel means fewer harmful greenhouse gases are created.

## Like a Greenhouse

The $CO_2$ that we pump into the air from our cars is causing a big problem. $CO_2$ is a greenhouse gas. Greenhouse gases are so-called because they make the atmosphere warmer, in the same way that a greenhouse keeps the air warm. Greenhouse gases are given off by human activity, such as burning fossil fuels. They encircle Earth like a warm blanket, which causes the planet to heat up. Earth is getting hotter and hotter. That is causing climate patterns to change. Climate change is one of the major threats facing our planet today.

Today, we are seeing more extreme weather in many parts of the world as a result of climate change. That weather includes **floods, droughts, hurricanes**, like the one shown right, and **wildfires**.

# CLIMATE CHANGE—WHAT'S GOING ON?

Climate change has always happened on Earth. It is the change in climate and the weather patterns the planet experiences. However, today climate change is accelerating, or speeding up, due to human activities. They include releasing harmful gases into Earth's atmosphere by burning fossil fuels.

# BIG POLLUTERS

It is not just the cars on our roads that are causing pollution. Every day, thousands of trucks drive along the highways and through our cities, transporting goods from one place to another. Those heavy vehicles have very big engines. Large engines burn a lot more fuel than smaller engines. They create a lot of harmful gases that pollute our atmosphere.

Dirty truck engines are creating an enormous amount of pollution.

## Deadly Diesel

Trucks do not run on gasoline. They run on diesel, another type of fuel. They can travel farther per gallon with diesel than with gasoline. However, burning diesel in an engine creates even more pollution than burning gasoline. In the United States in 2022, about 120 million gallons (454 million l) of diesel were used by vehicles—every day!

## Eco-Friendly Buses?

Using public transportation is a more eco-friendly choice than using your car. A bus carries more people and so reduces the number of cars on the road. However, buses are also contributing to the pollution on our roads and highways. Their engines also run on diesel, the dirtiest kind of fuel. They spew out harmful greenhouse gases, too.

# RAINING ACID

Car, truck, bus, and train engines emit, or give off, sulfur dioxide and nitrogen oxide gases into the air. When they mix with water and oxygen, they create acid rain. This is **toxic** rainwater. When it falls to Earth, it damages the soil and water by polluting them with its toxic content.

Trains are useful for carrying goods over long distances. They can have many cars and therefore can transport huge loads.

## Railroads Wrecking the Environment

The railroad network is essential for transporting goods and people. However, the trains used in the United States run on diesel fuel. In Europe, most rail networks have been converted to electric power. The trains get their power from overhead electric cables. They do not create any harmful gases. But that has not happened in the United States, and trains are still burning diesel fuel in their engines. To change the whole rail network to electric would be a huge job. Some new electric railroad lines are being opened, though.

## Cleaning Up Fuels

A lot of work is being done to create cleaner fuels. New fuels are being made from plant sources instead of from oil. They are called **biofuels**. They are usually made from corn or sugar cane. Biofuels are not fossil fuels, so they are sustainable when compared to oil. Burning them does not create the same pollution as burning gasoline or diesel. Biofuels can be mixed with regular gasoline to make it much cleaner. **Innovators** are also creating a new fuel to replace diesel altogether. It is called **liquefied natural gas (LNG)**. Although it is a fossil fuel, it creates less pollution than diesel.

9

# TAKING ECO ACTION:

# SHELL

One organization that is taking action against car pollution is Shell plc. This is a company that has been in business for a long time, taking oil and gas from the ground to create gasoline and diesel. Today, it is working hard to help clean up transportation. Shell has pledged, or promised, to become a net-zero emissions business by 2050. That means achieving a balance where the amount of carbon produced by the company and released into the atmosphere equals the amount it takes out of it.

## The Road to Net-Zero

To become a net-zero emissions business, Shell is reducing the emissions from its operations. It is also reducing emissions from the fuels and other products that it sells to customers. In addition, the company is using technology to capture and store any emissions that it does still produce.

Sugar cane grows best in tropical countries, such as Thailand. Sugar cane is a very productive biofuel crop. It produces eight times more energy than that required to grow it.

## FUEL OF THE FUTURE

In Singapore, Asia, Shell is transforming what was once an oil storage site and **refinery** into a state-of-the-art energy park. It is called Shell Energy and Chemicals Park Singapore. Here, the focus is on producing low-carbon energy. That includes biofuels. One exciting option that the park is exploring is turning the **hydrogen** made from materials such as used cooking oil and animal fats into low-carbon fuels. In the future, the fuel could be used to power the cars on our roads.

## Worldwide Work

Shell is focusing on producing innovative fuels that will help reduce emissions. They include biofuel, which is fuel made from plants and waste. The organization is working with people around the world to support them in this work. For example, in Brazil, Shell works with Raizen, a local company that creates biofuel from sugar cane. The biofuel produces almost 90 percent fewer harmful gases than gasoline.

## Powering Race Cars

In another exciting project, Shell is producing a new race fuel for the NTT INDYCAR SERIES. The product is made from ethanol —a sugarcane waste product—and other biofuels. It will be 100 percent renewable. The fuel will produce at least 60 percent fewer greenhouse gas emissions than gasoline. The ethanol used to create the fuel will be provided by Raizen, the Brazilian-based company that Shell is working with to create biofuel.

## Farther on Less Fuel

Shell is also supporting people who are working on making vehicles that are more efficient. Shell holds a competition every year: Shell Eco-marathon. To take part in the race, **engineers** form teams to design and build cars that can travel farther using less energy.

Once designed and built, Eco-marathon cars are taken to a track to test them and see which can travel the farthest using the least amount of energy.

# TAKE ECO ACTION
# TO CLEAN UP LAND TRAVEL

Companies like Shell are taking positive action against polluting transportation on our roads. And there are positive actions that you can take to cut back on the amount of pollution you contribute. By taking eco action, you will be playing an important part in helping to clean up transportation.

## Think Before You Travel

Before you travel, think! Is your car journey really necessary? Most car journeys are short—less than 2 miles (3.2 km), in fact. Many of them could be avoided, if we just think before we travel. Consider combining trips, so that you take fewer journeys each week. For example, you could add a shopping trip to another journey you really cannot avoid. If it's not your decision when to take the car, talk to your parents or guardians to help them make greener plans. You could keep a record of all the car journeys your family makes in a week. Then look at the list and see which you can cut.

## Share a Ride

For local journeys that many people are doing at the same time, why not share a ride? If you have to take the car to school, offer a ride to a local friend or two. Families can take turns being the driver. You can suggest that members of your family share rides to college or their places of work, as well. It saves fuel and cuts harmful gas emissions. And guess what? Those shared journey times can also be fun!

## On Your Bike!

For local trips, take a bike if you can. It is kind to the environment, and great for your fitness. Safety is very important on the roads. Remember to stay on safe roads and in bike lanes, and always wear a helmet.

## Take a Hike

We have two feet, so we should use them when we can! Plan your time, so you can replace short car journeys by walking instead. It may take a little longer, but there are big benefits to walking. You will notice things you never normally see, and get fit at the same time. And you will not be creating any pollution at all.

## Eco Action Wins

By changing your transportation habits, you'll help keep harmful gases from entering the air. And by using a bike or walking, you'll be reducing climate change and keeping yourself fit. Those are big wins for planet Earth—and for you, too!

ECO ACTION!

# CHAPTER 2

# PROBLEMS ON THE ROADS

Another big problem in road transportation today is **congestion**. That means roads that are too busy. There are too many vehicles on them, so the traffic cannot flow freely. Cars, buses, and trucks stand in the traffic with their engines running. They spew out pollution that contains greenhouse gases. That pollution also hangs in the air above the roads. It is breathed in by local people, and that causes serious health problems.

## An Invisible Danger

We cannot see most air pollution, but that does not mean it does not exist. The invisible threat is responsible for millions of deaths around the world every year. In 2022, air pollution caused more than 160,000 deaths in the world's five largest cities. More than 10 million people died across the world in that year as a result of air pollution. Road traffic makes a big contribution to this deadly problem.

When traffic cannot move freely on our roads and highways, pollution from vehicle exhausts becomes an even greater problem.

## Hurting People

Air pollution can cause many health problems in people. They may develop conditions such as asthma and bronchitis, which make it difficult to breathe. Air pollution has been linked to heart disease and cancer. It can also cause long-term problems with people's brains and other organs. The damage we are causing to ourselves by polluting our air is shocking. Millions of people are dying too early each year from diseases and conditions caused by air pollution.

## More Than Just a Waste of Time

If you have sat in the car in a traffic jam, you know how unpleasant it can be. You may be late for school or for an appointment. Perhaps you even miss a train or an airplane. You feel like you are wasting your time. It is also stressful. When congestion on the roads delays vehicles carrying out business, the effects can be even worse. If deliveries of materials are not made to a building site, for example, work cannot continue. If people do not reach a meeting, decisions cannot be made. Congestion costs us a lot every year. It has a harmful effect on our economic health, as well as on our physical well-being.

If you take a look at many driveways in the United States, you will see more than one car parked there. That level of car ownership is not sustainable for the future.

## SCARY NUMBERS

In 2020, there were about 287 million cars in the United States. And the scary thing is that this number is growing, not falling. In 2019, there were about 285 million cars in the country. More than 80 out of every 100 people in the United States owns a car. Since some people are too young or too old to own a car, that means many people own two or more cars. No wonder our roads are so congested! Things have to change.

# DIRTY STREETS

The most useful thing we can do to improve congestion in our towns and cities is to take vehicles off the roads. Congestion is especially bad at peak times in the morning and evening, as people travel to and from work. As a result, our journeys are delayed, and drivers and passengers are stressed. The air is full of harmful pollution, too. Some people say we should just build more roads to deal with the problem. But new roads just fill up with more vehicles, making congestion worse.

## Too Crowded

Most of our cities were designed a long time ago. The oldest ones were built before cars were even invented. Their streets are narrow, and there is not a lot of space for road users. In the last century, new cities were built with cars in mind. They had wide roads, so people could drive around the city center. But now that many more people live in cities, those roads have filled up with cars.

Modern cities such as New York City are packed with vehicles and people.

## CUT POLLUTION, SAVE LIVES

The World Health Organization (WHO) says that nine out of every 10 people in the world live in places where air pollution is too high. In 2021, the WHO released new guidelines on safe levels of air pollution. The guidelines recommended that the levels of air pollution allowed should be much lower. If governments take steps to reduce pollution to these new levels, many deaths can be prevented.

## It's Unhealthy

People need to get around cities by car. But they also need to get around on foot, and on bicycles. The congestion is causing bad air pollution for these road users. That harms their health. Breathing in polluted air can damage people's lungs. Asthma, an illness that makes it difficult for people to breathe easily, is most common in children. Living in a city with poor air quality makes asthma worse. Cities in the United States with high levels of asthma include Fresno in California, Tucson in Arizona, Richmond in Virginia, and Detroit in Michigan.

## Think of Cyclists

People are beginning to use bicycles and other cleaner forms of transportation more often. However, it is not pleasant to cycle through a city center with crowded roads and air pollution. It is too easy to have an accident in such heavy traffic. And breathing in the emissions can cause illness. It is better to have special lanes for cyclists, separate from the main traffic. They protect cyclists from being hit by cars and trucks. The air is also cleaner in those lanes.

As more people turn to cycling as a means of transportation, there is an even greater need to build more cycle lanes.

It is not just in wealthy countries such as the United States that congestion on the roads is a problem. Traffic jams are causing air pollution in cities all over the world. In low-income countries, the streets may be jammed with cars, bicycles, trucks, and animals. The roads are often poorly built and maintained, too. They may have holes, which makes driving on them difficult. That slows traffic, and causes further congestion. The problem is harming economies, because transportation cannot run smoothly. The biggest harm, however, is to people's health. Some of the cities with the most polluted air are in low-income countries, such as Lahore in Pakistan, and Dhaka in Bangladesh.

## So Many People

Many cities in low-income countries are very densely populated. That means a lot of people are crowded into the city. That makes problems of traffic congestion and air pollution much worse. The most densely populated city in the world is Manila, the capital of the Philippines, in Asia. It has 119,600 people living in each square mile. Compare that with New York City—the most densely populated city in the United States.

The streets of Dhaka are filled with cars, buses, and bicycle taxis called rickshaws.

# WORKING TOGETHER

In October 2021, the president of China, Xi Jinping, called on countries to work together to improve transportation around the world. He was speaking at the United Nations Global Sustainable Transport Conference. More than 1,000 people from more than 170 countries took part. President Xi also announced that China will set up a Global Innovation and Knowledge Center for Sustainable Transport, as a contribution to global transportation development.

The air pollution in Manila hangs over the city like a cloud.

New York City has about 27,500 residents in each square mile. Air pollution causes more than 4,000 deaths each year in Manila. During the Covid-19 **pandemic**, the amount of road traffic fell dramatically when people were forced to stay at home. For the first time in decades, the air became cleaner and the people of Manila could see the mountains that rise up beside their city.

## A Worldwide Solution

If we are going to solve the problems of climate change, the whole world is going to have to work together. Some countries have more money to spend on solving transportation problems than other countries do. But the pollution from a low-income country causes damage that affects people around the world. Wealthier countries need to help poorer countries improve their transportation networks. They can spend money on researching new ideas and cleaner technologies, for example. They can then share what they discover and help poorer countries make the changes that the whole world needs to see.

19

# TAKING ECO ACTION:

# ZIPCAR

One company tackling the problem of road traffic congestion is Zipcar. It is a fact that most cars are only used for a short time each day, or each week. For the rest of the time, they sit in the driveway, garage, or parking lot. The people who started Zipcar saw that this is very wasteful, and not sustainable. They believe that owning and using cars in that way cannot continue.

## Share a Car

We do need to have access to cars. They are an essential part of modern life. But we do not need access to the same car, all the time. We can share cars with other drivers. We can call up a car when we need one. Zipcar provides cars that sit on the streets or in garages in cities everywhere. They are there for sharing. Today, Zipcar is the largest car-sharing company in the world.

Zipcar can also be used by people driving for business. Business members can have many drivers included in their membership.

## SHARING THE IDEA OF CAR SHARING

The idea of car sharing started in Europe. An American named Robin Chase wanted to bring the idea to the United States. She founded Zipcar with her business partner Antje Danielson. They have won many awards for their work on reducing the number of cars on the road. The idea of cars on demand has really taken off. There are now many other businesses offering the same service.

## Made Easy by an App

How does Zipcar work? Zipcar is incredibly easy to use. You sign up to be a member, then use the app on your cell phone. You can hire a car or a van for a few minutes or hours, or for a day. You can book the vehicle in advance, or a few minutes before you want it. The rental cost includes gasoline. When you're ready to drive, the app shows you the vehicle's location. You also tap the app to unlock it.

## Planet-Friendly Parking

The people behind Zipcar think that each one of their cars takes 13 personally-owned vehicles off the road. That's reducing both congestion and pollution. Another helpful feature is that every Zipcar has its own reserved parking spot. Drivers know they can leave the car there. They do not have to circle the block looking for somewhere to park. That helps cut congestion and pollution, too.

## Farther to Go

Car sharing can make a big difference to congestion and pollution in city centers. But any car that runs on gasoline still creates pollution. Zipcar wants to go even further in cleaning up transportation. They are introducing electric cars to their fleet. They do not produce any harmful gases. Zipcar plans for all their cars to be electric by 2025.

Zipcar has led the way in introducing innovative car-sharing ideas to our towns and cities.

Own the trip, not the car®

How Zipcar works

Join

Drive

Return

# TAKE ECO ACTION
## AGAINST CONGESTION

Organizations such as Zipcar are taking positive action against the congestion on our roads and highways. And there are positive actions that you can take to get vehicles off the roads, too. You can reduce pollution and congestion. By taking eco action, you will be playing an important part in cleaning up transportation.

## Take the Train

Highways can get very congested at holiday times, when many people head out at the same time. For longer journeys, ask your family to think about taking the train and leaving the car at home. It's faster than traveling by car. It's also comfortable, and it's great to look out at the scenery. You can read or play games, or get something to eat. You will be helping the environment at the same time. That's a good choice!

## Choose Your Time

If you really have to drive in the city center, avoid the busiest times. They are in the morning and evening, when people travel to work and school. You are less likely to sit in traffic spewing out harmful emissions. Your journey will take less time and not be as stressful.

## Park Smart!

A lot of pollution and congestion is caused when drivers circle the streets, looking for a parking spot. Ask your parents or guardians to plan ahead, with a parking app on a cell phone. These apps can tell users where parking spots are available. They can then drive straight there. Maybe you live in the city center, and your parents or guardians have a parking spot that is empty during the day. Ask them to offer it to someone who needs it.

## Tell Others

Tell as many people as you can about the problems of congestion and pollution. Tell them about car-sharing choices such as Zipcar. Encourage members of your family to use car sharing for at least some of their journeys.

## Eco Action Wins

By using cleaner transportation and thinking about your journeys, you can reduce congestion on the roads. You will be making the air cleaner, and making all our streets more pleasant. And if you spread the word, more people will do the same. That will mean fewer cars on the roads, and quicker, less stressful journeys. Those are all big eco wins for planet Earth!

**ECO ACTION!**

# CHAPTER 3

# TROUBLE IN THE SKIES

It is not just our roads that present transportation challenges. Our skies are busier with airplanes than ever before. And that's a big problem, because air travel is a big polluter. It contributes up to 10 percent of the greenhouse gases that are harmful to our planet. That is because the powerful engines that move planes off the ground burn huge amounts of fuel. We urgently need to find ways to make air travel less polluting.

## On the Move

Air transportation is essential in our modern world. We may like to take a plane when we go on vacation, to experience new places and meet new people. Some people like to take many vacations each year. They have the time, and they want to see the world. But when everyone takes a plane on vacation, it contributes to the problem of air pollution. We need to change the way we travel. We have to take fewer flights.

The fuels used in aviation are not the same as the gasoline or diesel used by cars and trucks. Aviation fuels are especially dirty. Jet fuel releases $CO_2$ into the air when it is burned. It also releases other greenhouse gases.

## Making Problems

Flying for leisure is not the biggest use of planes. Every day, thousands of planes transport goods around the world. Almost everything that is made in a factory uses materials that come from more than one country. In the United States, for example, automobile parts are brought into the country from Mexico, Canada, China, Japan, Germany, South Korea, and other countries. Many of those materials arrive by plane. It is the same for many complex manufactured items. Factories do not want to store large amounts of materials. They are expensive, and they take up space, so the factories order just enough to last a short time. Then they order more. That creates even more flights across the world.

## Not-So-Good Business

The world of business is global. Millions of people travel the world by plane for meetings related to their work. They meet with their **suppliers**, or their customers. They meet up to discuss their research, or the problems they face. Meeting people in person can help build useful relationships in business. But all that traveling the world in planes is costing the planet too much.

Transporting goods around the world by air is causing enormous amounts of pollution to be pumped into the atmosphere.

# A LONG WAY TO GO

Aircraft travel farther on each journey than cars and trucks. That means they burn more fuel. Burning more fuel creates more $CO_2$ and other harmful gases. That is why air travel is making a real contribution to the warming of the atmosphere. There may be far fewer journeys by plane than by car, but each one has a greater impact.

# START AND STOP POLLUTION

Getting a heavy plane off the ground requires powerful engines. A flight is expensive to run. It therefore makes sense to take the fullest-possible load of people or goods on each one. Powerful airplane engines need a lot of fuel to give them enough power. Once a plane is flying at its regular **altitude**, the engines do not have to work quite so hard. Fuel consumption is stable. But when it is time to land, the engines have to work harder again. They then burn more fuel, and create more harmful emissions.

## Frightening Flights

Each year, we are taking more and more flights. In the past few decades, the number of flights taken has increased a lot. In 2019, almost 39 million flights were made. More than 4 billion people traveled as passengers. All that flying has had a bad effect on the atmosphere. Since the 1980s, the level of emissions from aviation has doubled. We cannot afford to go on like this. We have to find ways to reduce the amount of air travel around the world.

The noise pollution and air pollution from airplanes can be damaging to people's health. Many people who live in houses over which airplanes regularly fly find the noise pollution stressful.

## Short but Harmful

Many plane journeys are quite short. They are called short-haul flights. Planes fly from one part of a country to another. The journey can be just a few hundred miles, but are the worst kinds of flights. The most pollution happens when a plane takes off and lands. So having many short-haul flights creates a lot of pollution. People often take short-haul flights for their work. They fly to a meeting, then home again. It is important to find other methods of travel for these journeys. A train ride takes a bit longer, but it creates much less pollution. Another alternative is not to travel and meet online instead.

# STINGS IN THE TRAILS

The wispy white trails we see across the sky behind airplanes are also a problem. They are ice **particles** created by the exhaust of the engines. New research shows they are also contributing to **global warming**. They add to the blanket effect caused by natural clouds. That raises the temperature of the atmosphere.

The white trails left behind an airplane as it flies through the sky are adding to the heat that is causing our planet to warm.

## Trouble Where People Live

Another problem with short-haul flights is that they often take off from smaller airports. These are often located very close to where people live. When planes take off and land so near to people's homes, they pollute the air that residents breathe and are very noisy. That is very harmful to people's health.

## Pollution Hotspots

All the buildings and supplies that come with air travel contribute to air pollution, too. Airports must take many deliveries of fuel each day. Mostly, they arrive in large, polluting tanker trucks. Passengers arrive at airports in polluting cars. Many airport vehicles drive around, transporting people, luggage, and goods. Such activities make airports centers of pollution. Thankfully, many airports are now starting to use electric vehicles.

# TAKING ECO ACTION:

# THE INTERNATIONAL AIR TRANSPORT ASSOCIATION

One organization trying to tackle the problem of aviation pollution is the International Air Transport Association (IATA). The members of IATA are the airlines of the world. These airlines carry goods as well as passengers. They are now fully on board with making change happen. In 2021, IATA agreed that the amount of $CO_2$ created by their planes should be massively cut by 2050. There are several ways they plan to make this happen.

## Making New Fuels

The biggest way to cut $CO_2$ emissions from aviation is to use a cleaner fuel. New fuels are being invented that are not made from petroleum. Sustainable aviation fuel (SAF) is a biofuel made from sustainable feedstocks. They are cooking oil and other waste oils from animals and plants. Food scraps and forestry waste can also be used to make SAF. SAF is mixed half-and-half with regular fuel. The result is a fuel that creates fewer harmful emissions. IATA members are trying to use more SAF in their planes, but it is more expensive than regular fuel. Far more SAF needs to be produced for it to become cheaper.

If all planes refueled with SAF before they took off, air pollution would be greatly reduced.

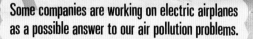

Some companies are working on electric airplanes as a possible answer to our air pollution problems.

## Better Design

IATA airlines are also looking at new designs for their planes. Researchers are finding new ways to make planes burn less fuel when they fly. They can be designed so they travel through the air more efficiently. Small changes to the design of wings or the plane body can make a big difference. The design of the engine is very important, too. The seats and other fittings inside can be made of lighter materials to make planes lighter. Lighter planes burn less fuel, and so produce less pollution.

## Better Planning

IATA airplane operators can plan their flights better. They can be smarter about how many planes are flying at one time. They can reduce the overall number of journeys, while carrying the same loads. Airports can do the same. Electric vehicles can be used to transport passengers, luggage, and goods around the site, for example.

## GOING ELECTRIC?

Can we replace fueled aircraft with planes that run on electricity? That is the big question for aviation, and for IATA members. Electric vehicles take their power from a battery onboard. This battery stores electricity. Planes travel farther than cars, so they use more energy. They need batteries that can store a lot of energy to travel a long distance. That is why electric planes are most suitable for shorter journeys. Electric planes will certainly be used on short-haul flights in the future.

# TAKING ECO ACTION:

# THE SOLAR IMPULSE FOUNDATION

More than 20 years ago, one man had a vision for the future. He was Bertrand Piccard from Switzerland, the founder of the Solar Impulse Foundation. His dream was to fly around the world without using a single drop of fuel. In 1999, he had traveled right around the world in a hot air balloon. It was fueled by gas. At the end of his adventure, he decided to try to make the same journey without any fossil fuels. He wanted to show the world a new way forward.

## Power of the Sun

Bertrand Piccard teamed up with André Borschberg, an engineer. They wanted to create a plane that would be powered only by the energy from the sun. Their plane would fly around the world, day and night, without fuel. They worked hard on designing their solar-powered plane. In 2010, they made their first night-time flight. The plane flew on energy stored in its battery, and the flight was a success!

Solar Impulse's combination of state-of-the-art **solar panels** and lightweight materials allow it to fly for long periods of time powered only by the sun.

# SPECIAL THROUGH SOLAR

The top of the Solar Impulse plane is covered in solar panels. They convert sunlight into electricity. Its wingspan is wider than a jumbo jet, but it weighs about the same as a family car. At night, it uses electricity stored during the day in its battery. Its top speed is just 60 miles per hour (96.6 kph), but it can fly for several days.

## Around the World

More tests followed. Then in 2015, the around-the-world flight began for Bertrand and André. Starting in Abu Dhabi in the Middle East, the Solar Impulse took off on the first stage of its flight. When it crossed the Pacific Ocean, it remained in the air for longer than any aircraft in history. It flew for more than five days and five nights. Over the total around-the-world trip, the plane flew about 25,000 miles (40,234 km) without a single drop of fuel. The extraordinary journey was watched with wonder by the world. It showed how aviation could be changed.

## Making It Happen

Since that amazing flight, the Solar Impulse Foundation has continued its work. Today, it advises governments and others about ways to improve the sustainability of our world. It has found more than 1,000 eco-action ideas that could work. It is working with politicians, **economists**, and business leaders to make change happen. It wants the leaders in all these fields to work together. It is clear that only through cooperation can we fight climate change.

Bertrand Piccard described his flight across the Pacific Ocean: "I flew on as if in a dream. The elements escorted me peacefully and the course of time disappeared. I could have stayed there forever, between the sun and the clouds, the moon and the ocean."

# AGAINST AIR POLLUTION

Organizations like the Solar Impulse Foundation are taking positive action to clean up air transportation. The people behind the organization truly want everyone to believe that new technologies can make a big difference. And there are positive actions that you can take to help tackle this important issue, too. By taking these eco actions, you'll be helping the planet and the people, plants, and animals that live on it.

## Cut Food Miles

Food miles are the miles traveled by food from where it is produced to where it is sold. People may enjoy eating **exotic** fruits all year round, and other foods that are never grown in our own country. But planes and ships bring them to us from many miles away. Each one is adding to the pollution of our world, and contributing to climate change.

## Shop Smart

It is time to think before we buy and to shop smart. When you choose fruits and vegetables, think about where they were grown. How far have they traveled, and how did they reach your store? Leave the produce from the other side of the world on the shelf. If everyone stops buying it, the store will stop stocking it.

## Eat with the Seasons

Find out which foods are produced locally to you at each time of year. Some produce is grown locally in just one season. If you eat it in a different season, it has traveled farther to reach you. Once you know about what's in season, tell everyone about it! Especially tell the people who buy the food for your family, or for your school. Learn when foods are in season with the Seasonal Food Guide online. The website address for this resource is on page 47.

## Take a Staycation

A staycation is a vacation taken close to home. You don't have to take a long flight or car journey to have a great vacation. Many people took staycations during the Covid-19 pandemic. They could not fly abroad or travel far. As a result, the skies were cleaner, and everyone still had a great time.

## Change Business

Do you know people who travel by plane on business? Ask them if they could have their meetings online instead. Tell them you care about the damage that planes are doing to our world. Remind them that short-haul flights cause the worst pollution.

## Eco Action Wins

Buying goods that are produced in your home country will help reduce aviation pollution. Buying foods that are grown locally and are in season reduces food miles. That helps reduce climate change. Telling others about what you have learned will help them to shop smart, too. If you take as few flights as possible, it will help clean up our skies. Those are all eco wins for planet Earth!

ECO ACTION!

# CHAPTER 4

# POLLUTING THE OCEANS

Every day, thousands of huge **cargo** ships carry goods around the world. Transporting goods and people by sea is kinder to the environment than making those journeys by truck or plane. However, the massive amount of shipping traffic across the world still has a huge impact. More than 90 percent of world trade is carried across the oceans. It travels in around 90,000 **marine** vessels. Those vessels burn fossil fuels in their engines. Although they are traveling far out at sea, a long way from people, their effect on the world is felt by everyone.

## A Cycle of Damage

The fuel in the engines of the **container ships** that cross our oceans is very dirty. When it is burned, it gives off a lot of $CO_2$. That collects in the atmosphere and creates warming. That dirty fuel also gives off other gases that create harmful pollution. They gather in the air, then fall back to Earth as acid rain. Acid rain harms the plants and animals living where it falls. It gets into the ground and pollutes the water.

The ships that crisscross our oceans pump out harmful pollution as they travel, further damaging the planet.

Ocean animals, such as humpback whales, are harmed by the pollution that ships discharge into the water.

# PROBLEMS WITH PORTS

Just as airports are hubs of aviation pollution, ports are centers of shipping pollution. Wherever container ships arrive to load and unload their cargo, they are polluting the air and the water. Their engines spew fumes into the air. They also discharge, or let out, harmful waste chemicals into the water. All the vehicles used to transport the goods on land to and from the ports are polluters, too.

## Hurting the Oceans

The substances given off by the engines of container ships also pollute the oceans. The harmful gases get into the water and harm the wildlife there. The ships also release their waste into the oceans, which harms the marine life. Altogether, shipping is causing too much damage to our world.

## So Much Traffic

There is no sign that the damage we are causing to the oceans is going to stop. The amount of shipping across our oceans is growing each year. It is the scale of shipping that makes it such a big contributor to global warming and climate change. In fact, if global shipping were a country, it would be the sixth-largest producer of greenhouse gas emissions in the world! Yet, there have been few controls on the amount of $CO_2$ that can be emitted from ships. Experts think that the amount of harmful emissions from shipping will increase greatly over the next few decades. That is because we want to transport more and more goods. In fact, the emissions could become much higher than they are today if we do nothing to solve this serious problem. It is clear that we need to take urgent action.

# DAMAGING OUR OCEANS

The huge container ships that cross the oceans are not only creating pollution in the air. They are releasing substances into the water that are damaging the living things found there. In fact, all big ships contribute to this pollution. The huge cruise ships that take people on vacations around the world are doing the same thing. All these vessels need to clean up their act, so we can protect our marine life.

A cleanup operation after an oil spill at sea can take months.

## Dirty Water

Large ships pollute ocean waters in many ways. They carry huge amounts of water in the bottom of their **hulls**. The water is to help keep the ship stable in the ocean and is called ballast water. It needs to be cleared out of the hull regularly, and replaced. That water is released into an ocean, river, or lake. The problem is that it can contain harmful substances, such as oils and other chemicals. These are bad for the animals in the water. The water can also contain species of plants and animals from other countries where it was picked up. These can cause problems when these species invade the waterways they are dumped into.

## Cruising Along

Cruise ships are some of the worst polluters in the oceans. They create huge amounts of polluted water. All the water that is used onboard for daily operations such as washing, flushing the toilets, and cooking in the kitchens, is released into the ocean. They also release a lot of other waste, such as packaging and plastics.

Creatures in the ocean, such as turtles and fish, become tangled in packaging and plastics, and die. The waste materials can also cause tiny plants called **algae** to grow on the water. Millions of algae join together to form a layer over the water's surface. The layer stops light and air from penetrating the water. That kills the animals and plants living below the surface.

## Hit at Sea

The other way in which ships harm marine life is simply by bumping into it. Huge container ships and cruise ships regularly hit whales and other large animals as they cross the oceans. The creatures are almost always killed.

# SPILLING OIL

People around the world need oil, and huge oil tanker ships carry it from country to country. Sometimes, the ships have accidents. They split open, and millions of gallons of oil spill out into the ocean. The damage this causes is truly terrible. Fish and seabirds become covered in oil and die. Coastlines and beaches are covered in it, too. It can take decades to clean up after these disasters. If we can use less oil in future, there should be fewer of these terrible accidents at sea.

This bird is covered in oil from a spill. Many birds covered in oil will try to clean it off with their beaks. That results in the birds swallowing the toxic oil which can kill them.

# TAKING ECO ACTION:

# OCEANBIRD

The good news is that many organizations involved with ocean transportation are coming to Earth's rescue. They include the two companies that are working together on Oceanbird, a completely new type of cargo ship, powered only by the wind. Just as the wind helped us explore Earth centuries ago, the people developing this modern-day vessel believe it can help us now preserve our precious planet.

## Ships to the Rescue

Oceanbird is being developed by two companies in Sweden. They are called Alfa Laval and Wallenius. The dream of the developers is to make shipping sustainable. The technology in Oceanbird makes it possible to power the largest ocean-going vessels over long distances without polluting the planet. They can travel for a long time, as long as the wind is blowing. And it is very windy out on the oceans!

Oceanbird's sails allow it to capture the energy of the wind to drive it forward.

## How Does It Work?

Oceanbird has massive "wing sails" on deck. Each one is 260 feet (79.3 m) high, and made from metal, so it is strong. These huge masts make Oceanbird the tallest ship in the world. They can be lowered, too, if necessary. A computer on board controls the position of the sails, so they can move to catch as much wind as possible as the ship travels across the ocean. The ship will also have an engine to help it get into and out of harbors and ports. It will be powered by clean energy.

## Slow and Steady

Oceanbird can carry a lot of cargo. It travels slowly but cleanly. It can carry 7,000 cars, at a speed of 11 miles per hour (17.7 kph). It can cross the Atlantic Ocean in 12 days. A fuel-powered ship takes about eight days. Using the power of the wind instead of regular fuel to make the journey will be so much cleaner. The people making Oceanbird say it will create 90 percent fewer emissions than a regular container vessel.

Oceanbird is a huge vessel. It is 650 feet (198 m) long and 344 feet (105 m) high.

# JUST THE BEGINNING

Oceanbird has not yet set sail, but there are hopes it will be in use by 2024. The vessel is a cargo ship, but it's just the start of the story. The technology in Oceanbird can be used for ships of all types, such as cruise ships. The people at Oceanbird want to be part of a solution to the problem of global warming and climate change. They also want to inspire others to do the same. They believe this is the beginning of a new era for global transportation.

# TAKE ECO ACTION
# AGAINST SHIPPING POLLUTION

The creators of Oceanbird are taking positive action against the pollution caused by global shipping. And there are positive actions that you can take, too. By taking these eco actions, you'll be helping to clean up the atmosphere. You will also be helping to clean up the water in our oceans. That will mean a better, brighter future for our planet and its people.

## Choose Carefully

We are the consumers of the goods that are shipped around the world in polluting vessels. We can all make a difference by thinking carefully about what we consume. Choose goods that are made close to where you live, if you can. Carry out research. Find out about where the things you buy are made. If you discover they are shipped around the world, you could look for a more local choice instead. Supporting local businesses is good for the planet.

## Reduce Waste

About one-third of all the food we produce is wasted. A lot of foods are transported round the world by ships. That is especially the case for foods that last a long time on the shelf. Think about the journey your food has taken. Do not buy more than you need. If you no longer need it, give it to someone who does.

## Campaign Against Climate Change

Make your voice heard! Join an organization that is helping to raise awareness of climate change. Take part in any events that they hold to tell the world about this issue. The more people speak up about climate change, the more likely governments will be to take action.

## Eco Action Wins

By thinking carefully about what you buy, you'll help tackle the problem of shipping pollution. Buying goods that are produced locally will reduce the miles they need to be transported. It will help your local producers to stay in business, too. Buying only what you need will mean fewer journeys are taken to get the goods to you. Those are all great eco wins for planet Earth and its people.

ECO ACTION!

# A CLEANER FUTURE

We have seen how transportation is contributing to the problem of global warming and climate change. Many people around the world are working on ways to solve the problem. They are inventing smart technologies that use cleaner fuels. They are even finding ways to leave oil-based fuels behind forever.

## New Power for Cars

Electric cars are becoming more common on our roads. As they become cheaper, and there are more places to **recharge** them, more people will switch to electric. Some people are working on cars that will hardly need to plug into the electrical **power grid** at all. They will be covered in solar panels and powered by sunshine. The car giant Ford has produced a trial car with solar panels on the roof. As it drives around in the sunshine, it makes its own electricity from the panels—enough to run the car for about four hours. That idea is an exciting look at the way forward.

In the Netherlands, the trains run on electricity. All the electricity that powers the trains comes from wind power. No fossil fuels are used to create the power, and that means no harmful emissions are given off.

Filling stations will have pumps for filling car tanks with hydrogen. The only emissions that hydrogen cars emit is water vapor, which is harmless.

## Help from Hydrogen

The other big development in vehicle fuel is hydrogen. Hydrogen is a gas, and it contains a lot of energy. Using it to power vehicles does not produce any harmful emissions. Hydrogen is not burned in a car's engine. It is used in a **hydrogen fuel cell** inside the car to make electricity. The cell powers an electric motor that drives the vehicle. People fill up the tank with hydrogen at a filling station. That's much quicker than waiting for an electric battery to recharge. Trial hydrogen cars are already being tested on the roads.

## Cutting Congestion

It's good news that there are measures that can reduce pollution. But we can only reduce congestion by taking vehicles off the road. There are many ideas for new forms of transportation in cities. They include flying taxis. These electric vehicles take off and land vertically. They would use a network of mini "skyports" located in places where people live and work. A California-based firm, Joby Aviation, is leading in this area. It has carried out more than 1,000 test flights, and hopes to begin operating in 2024. Another idea is to reduce the congestion caused by delivery vehicles by using flying drones.

## A Brighter Future

The Covid-19 pandemic showed that when vehicles are taken off the road, air quality improves very quickly. Families, businesses, and governments now understand that we need to make that change happen for good. We are all beginning to change our behavior. We have better technology than ever before to help us make those changes. We all need to take eco action now and invest in smart science and sustainable living. Together, we can clean up our transportation networks and build a brighter, better future for our world.

# BUILD A CAREER IN
# ECO ACTION

Why not take more eco action, and develop a career in cleaning up transportation? There are many different career paths that you can explore. And they will all help us all move toward a cleaner future. Imagine the difference your generation could make to Earth by making a career out of eco action! Here are just some of the areas that you could explore.

## Get into Eco Food

If you care about reducing food miles, and helping local producers, you could set up a food store in your community. Or it could be a café or restaurant. Sell only foods that are in season and produced in the local area. They will have few food miles. You will enjoy working with farmers and other food producers. And you will love talking to your customers and showing them how they are making a difference. Studying subjects at school such as business, math, and food science could help you in this eco-friendly career choice.

## Get into Engineering

Do you want to invent the technologies of the future that can help clean up our transportation? You could work for an energy company that is developing cleaner fuels. Or you could work for an engineering design company that is developing completely new ideas, such as wind power for modern container ships. You will need a good understanding of science for these roles. Studying subjects at school and college such as math, physics, chemistry, and engineering will help you get into these careers.

If you get into engineering, you'll be able to help redesign our future into one that is more protective of our planet.

## Spread the Word

Perhaps your skills are in communication. The world needs people who are passionate about the need to clean up our transportation. If you love writing about things that matter to you, you could train as a journalist. You can write for national or local newspapers and magazines. You can start your own website and write blogs for your followers. Studying subjects at school such as English, information technology (IT), and social science are helpful for careers in journalism.

## Get into Politics

If you want to change policy decisions on eco issues such as transportation, why not become a change-maker? Be one of the people making the decisions. You can represent the people in your local district. Maybe one day you will represent your state. Most people working in politics started in their local area. Join your local party, or a group wanting to make the same changes as you. Learn how to organize a campaign. Small campaigns can lead to bigger ones! Studying subjects at school such as English, history, social sciences, and math are helpful for finding future jobs in politics.

Make your voice heard by becoming a campaigner for eco action.

# GLOSSARY

**algae** green organisms that grow on the water's surface

**altitude** height above the ground

**atmosphere** the layer of gases that surrounds Earth

**biofuels** fuels from renewable sources, such as sugar cane, which can be blended into gasoline and diesel

**cargo** goods transported on a ship or plane

**climate** the regular weather conditions of an area

**congestion** when there is too much traffic on roads for it to flow freely

**container ships** large ships that carry many containers of goods

**diesel** a vehicle fuel made from oil

**droughts** periods of time with little or no rain

**economists** people whose work is to study the economy

**emissions** substances discharged into the air by something, such as machinery

**engineers** People who design and build things such as machines

**environment** a natural place that surrounds plants and animals

**exotic** not found locally, unusual

**floods** the movement of large amounts of water over land that is normally dry

**fossil fuels** fuels such as coal, oil, and gas that were made from animals and plants that died long ago

**gasoline** a vehicle fuel made from oil

**global warming** an increase in Earth's temperatures, caused by human actions

**greenhouse gases** gases that trap heat and send it back to Earth

**hulls** the outer, watertight bodies of boats or ships

**hurricanes** powerful storms with heavy rain and strong winds

**hydrogen** a gas that can be extracted from water

**hydrogen fuel cell** a device that combines hydrogen and oxygen to create electricity and water

**innovators** people who introduce smart new ideas or ways of doing something

**liquefied natural gas (LNG)** a new fuel for powering ships made by cooling natural gas until it becomes a liquid

**marine** of or relating to the oceans

**pandemic** a disease that affects a number of parts of the world

**particles** tiny, often microscopic, pieces

**polluting** adding toxic substances

**pollution** harmful substances in the air, land, or water

**power grid** the network that distributes electricity from power stations to consumers

**recharge** to top up with energy

**refinery** a place in which oil found in its natural state is turned into fuel such as gasoline

**solar panels** panels made of substances that can collect the energy in sunlight to turn it into electricity

**suppliers** people or organizations that supply goods or materials

**sustainable** can be relied on for the foreseeable future

**toxic** poisonous

**wildfires** large fires that spread quickly through natural areas

# FIND OUT MORE

## Books

Chandler, Matt. *The Tech Behind Electric Cars* (Tech on Wheels). North Mankato, MN: Capstone Press, 2019.

Rebman, Nick. *Earth-Friendly Transportation* (Helping the Environment). Mendota Heights, MN: North Star Editions, 2021.

Schilke, Brett. *Journey to City X: Adventures in Engineering for Kids* (Design Genius Junior). Beverly, MA: Rockport Publishers, 2020.

## Websites

Find out about the work of the Solar Impulse Foundation at:
**https://aroundtheworld.solarimpulse.com/img/pdf/SI_FOR_KIDS.pdf**

Calculate your food miles at:
**www.bbc.com/future/bespoke/follow-the-food/calculate-the-environmental-footprint-of-your-food.html**

Find out lots more about careers in conservation at:
**www.environmentalscience.org/careers**

Learn about Alice, the world's first all-electric commuter aircraft:
**www.eviation.com**

Find out how you can eat in-season food with the Seasonal Food Guide:
**www.seasonalfoodguide.org**

Find out more about the design of Oceanbird at:
**www.theoceanbird.com**

**Publisher's note to educators and parents:**
All the websites featured above have been carefully reviewed to ensure that they are suitable for students. However, many websites change often, and we cannot guarantee that a site's future contents will continue to meet our high standards of educational value. Please be advised that students should be closely monitored whenever they access the Internet.

# INDEX

## About the Author

Robyn Hardyman has written many books for children that look at the problems that affect our planet today. In writing this book, she has learned how important it is that we all take eco action and make the changes needed to reduce transportation problems to help clean up our planet.